Another 101 Drills to Improve Your Golf Game

Glenn Berggoetz
Alan Moyer

©2004 Coaches Choice. All rights reserved. Printed in the United States.

No part of this book may be reproduced, stored in a retrieval system, or transmitted, in any form or by any means, electronic, mechanical, photocopying, recording, or otherwise, without the prior permission of Coaches Choice. Throughout this book, the masculine shall be deemed to include the feminine and vice versa.

ISBN: 1-58518-894-8
Library of Congress Control Number: 2004104670
Cover design: Jeanne Hamilton
Book design: Jeanne Hamilton
Photos: Don Hangartner
Front cover photo: Don Hangartner

Coaches Choice
P.O. Box 1828
Monterey, CA 93942
www.coacheschoice.com

Dedication

To Brian Berggoetz—the best golfer in the family and a great brother.

—Glenn

To Lauren, Allison, and Jeffrey.

—Alan

Acknowledgments

Special thanks go to Barry Christen, Leo Cornewell, Dawn Crocker, Driving with Our Eyes Shut, Tom "Lovenuts" Dwyer, Sally Hangartner, Coralea Hart, Joel & the 'Bots, Becki McCall, Kelly Mettert and Keith Petre at Custom Golf of New Haven, Ian Price and Cleveland Golf, John Rang and the entire gang at Bobick's Golf, Jim Sprinkle, Terrance & Phillip, TV's Frank & Dr. F, and Willow Bend Country Club.

Contents

Dedication 3
Acknowledgments 4
Introduction 6
Part I – Full-Swing Drills
    Chapter 1   Address Position 9
    Chapter 2   Backswing 13
    Chapter 3   Swing Path 27
    Chapter 4   Weight Shift 41
    Chapter 5   Impact Position 59
    Chapter 6   Release 67
    Chapter 7   General 79
Part II – Short-Game Drills
    Chapter 8   Around the Green 99
    Chapter 9   Putting 113
About the Authors 126

Introduction

The golf swing is a wondrous thing. We are all in search of finding the perfect swing that will work for us. And while that perfect swing varies from person to person, all great swings share some common denominators.

By providing you with 101 drills that cover all aspects of the golf game, we are giving you the information you need to find your perfect swing. More importantly, we are providing you with the drills that will allow you to get the ball in the hole in the fewest strokes possible.

Possibly the best thing you can do to improve your golf game is to see yourself swing. Golfers are often shocked at what they see the first time they get to take a look at their swing. And while it is best that you get to watch your swing while under the guidance of a competent teaching professional, the simple act of borrowing a video camera and getting a friend to videotape some swings can do wonders. Watching a few swings will reveal to you what swing flaws you might have, and this book will provide you with the drills to correct those flaws.

Golf is fun. And it's especially fun when you play well. Use this book wisely, and you'll play the best golf of your life.

PART I

Full-Swing Drills

1

Address Position

Drill #1

Problem: Poor posture

Poor posture at address almost assures you of hitting a poor shot. If you have problems with your posture, do the following: Stand as if you were preparing to return a serve in tennis. Your back is straight, your knees are flexed, you're bent slightly at the waist, and your butt is sticking out a little bit—a good athletic position. Now let your arms fall in front of you and bring your palms together. Finally, have someone put a club in your hands. Now you're ready to swing.

Drill #2

Problem: Poor alignment

Assume your normal address position, and then take your left hand off the club and point to a spot that is 10 yards to the left of your target line (if you're right-handed). Holding your arm in that position, check to see that the heels of your feet, your thighs, and your shoulders are all lined up with your extended left arm. If they aren't, adjust them so they are.

2

Backswing

Drill #3

Problem: Cocking wrists immediately upon beginning take-away

If your first movement on your take-away is to cock your wrists, do this drill. Take your address position, but choke down on the club so the butt end of the grip is poking you in the belly button. From this position, begin your take-away, making sure you keep the grip end of the club in your belly button, and the club at a 90-degree angle to your midsection. When you can consistently and comfortably do this, you've taken a huge stride towards developing a solid take-away.

Drill #4

Problem: Poor take-away

To help get a feel for the one-piece take-away in which your entire body works together, take your address position with your hands choked way down on the club, and the butt end of the grip sticking in your front armpit. From that position, begin your swing, noticing how your entire body—shoulders, arms, hips, and legs—is forced to move in unison. This united movement is what you want to attain and feel every time you begin your swing.

Drill #5

Problem: Poor take-away

If you have a problem with either picking the club straight up immediately upon beginning your backswing or with snapping the club to the inside, do this drill. Using a long-iron, address a ball. Place a second ball 12 inches behind the ball you are addressing. As you begin your swing, focus on brushing away the second ball with a long, low take-away.

Drill #6

Problem: Taking club away to the inside

Stand on one side of a bench with the clubhead on the ground on the other side of the bench. From that position, take your backswing, allowing the bench to force you to take the club straight down your target line for the first few feet of your take-away.

Drill #7

Problem: Not completing backswing

Stand about a foot away from a wall with your back to the wall. Hold your hands at chest level with your fingers extended and your palms facing out. From this position, rotate your torso so your palms touch the wall in back of you. Focus on keeping your feet planted and on rotating your shoulders, not your hips, to make sure you can touch the wall.

Drill #8

Problem: Not completing backswing

To get a good idea of what a full completed backswing feels like, address a ball with your stance narrowed by six to ten inches, and with your rear foot pulled back six to eight inches. Now swing. Notice how this address position allows your shoulders to rotate more easily.

After you get a good feel for the full shoulder turn you're developing, modify your stance to just four inches narrower than usual, and only pull your rear foot back three inches. When you can comfortably make a full, completed backswing from this address position, go back to your normal stance.

Drill #9

Problem: Not completing backswing

To get a good visual image of yourself getting a good shoulder turn on your backswing and coming to a full, completed backswing position, take your address position while holding a club across your shoulders. From this address position, swing to the top of your backswing, and check to see if the club is pointing directly over the ball you've addressed. If it is, you've made a full turn at the top of your backswing.

Drill #10

Problem: Right elbow flies out at top of backswing

To rectify this problem, take some practice swings in which you grip the club with your hands split two to three inches apart. When you swing using this split-grip technique, it is virtually impossible to let your right elbow fly out at the top of your backswing.

When it feels comfortable swinging in this manner, go ahead and hit a few balls while still using the split-grip technique. Be sure to take smooth, fluid swings when swinging this way.

Drill #11

Problem: Club gets off-line at top of backswing

Take your address position, and have a friend stand about eight or ten feet away, lined up with your heels. From that position, begin your swing, stopping when you get to the top of your backswing. Now check to see if your club is pointing directly at your friend. If it's not pointing directly at your friend, have your friend move you so you are in the proper position, and hold that position for a few seconds to get a feel for where your body should be. Repeat the drill until you can consistently get the club on-line at the top of your backswing. Make sure that when you do this drill, you never finish your swing and hit the ball, unless you enjoy sending your friends to the hospital.

Drill #12

Problem: Head moves vertically during backswing

It's quite natural for your head to move laterally a little bit during your swing, but moving your head up and down is a death move. To help correct up-and-down movement, put a tee in your mouth with the point of it sticking out. Now address the ball and make sure the tee is pointing directly at your target line or the ball. Begin your swing and stop at the top of your backswing. The tee should still be pointing directly at your target line. If it points above your target line, you're raising up; if it points below your target line, you're dipping down. Once you get to where you point at your target line with the tee on every backswing, go ahead and swing through to your impact position, stopping at impact to check to see that the tee is again pointing directly at your target line.

Drill #13

Problem: Too much lower-body movement during backswing

The more moving parts you have during your swing, the easier it is for one of those parts to get in the wrong position and cause you to hit an errant shot. If your lower body is moving too much, try this simple drill.

Take your address position with your front foot turned out at a 90-degree angle. Now swing. Notice how this simple adjustment to your address position locks up your lower body and allows very little movement from your waist down. This quiet lower body is what you want to attain with every swing.

Drill #14

Problem: Arms wrap around head at top of backswing

When your arms wrap around your head at the top of your backswing, you lose extension and cut down on your swing arc, costing you a tremendous amount of distance. To correct this problem, take some swings with your hands split three inches apart on the grip. This grip will make it much more difficult for your elbows to collapse, which will keep your hands out away from your body, and allow you to create a big swing arc. When it feels comfortable taking practice swings this way, go ahead and hit some balls using this grip.

3

Swing Path

Drill #15

Problem: Coming over the top

To cure that over-the-top move in which your front shoulder opens up too early, address a ball in which you line up your body 45 to 60 degrees left of your target (if you're right-handed). The key with the alignment is to make sure you not only open up your front foot, but also turn your back foot so it is angled 45 to 60 degrees left of your target.

From this address position, hit the ball to your target. You will immediately notice that the only way to get the ball to fly close to your target is to come from a severely inside swing path. As you get accustomed to this swing, alter your address position so you are angled only 30 degrees left of your target, and hit some balls using this stance. Eventually, return to your normal address position and hit balls, focusing on maintaining that inside-to-inside swing path feel you have developed.

Drill #16

Problem: Coming over the top

To force yourself to come from an inside swing path as you attack the ball, place a tee 18 inches behind your ball, making sure the tee is in line with your target line. The tee should stick out of the ground at least two inches. Now proceed to take your swing, focusing on missing the tee by coming at the ball from an inside swing path. Don't concern yourself with ball flight—you're only concerned with developing an inside-to-inside swing path. When you get to the point where you can consistently come inside of the tee without hitting it, move it a couple inches closer to the ball, and repeat the drill.

Drill #17

Problem: Coming over the top

To get a feel for coming at the ball from an inside swing path, do an exaggerated imitation of Jim Furyk's swing. Start by taking your normal address position, then, on the take-away, take the club back to the far outside of your target line. From that position, loop the club back around to an exaggerated inside position where you drop your elbow excessively into the slot, then complete your swing.

Don't expect to get this swing down on the first try. But after a few efforts, you'll find it isn't too difficult. You will also probably notice that you are hitting the ball better than you expected, and that you are getting a lot better distance on your shots as well.

As this swing becomes more comfortable and as you can better feel yourself coming from an inside swing path, gradually alter your swing back to taking the club away down the target line, and approaching the impact zone from a less exaggerated inside swing path.

Drill #18

Problem: Coming over the top

To get yourself to come from an inside swing path, stick a long pencil in the ground two inches in back of a ball and about a quarter of an inch outside the far edge of the ball. You also want to angle the pencil about 20 degrees towards you. Now swing, focusing on coming at the ball from the inside so your clubhead slides right under the pencil.

Drill #19

Problem: Spinning out

When your front shoulder opens up before you make contact with the ball, you've spun out. To remedy this swing flaw, take some swings where you keep your front heel off the ground throughout your entire swing. Swing easily at first until you become comfortable with the alteration. Focus on how swinging in this manner feels different from your normal swing.

Drill #20

Problem: Casting the club

To make sure you hold the angle formed by your arms and the club as you approach the impact zone, get out a wood or a long-iron, and tee a ball up high. Now, instead of taking your normal address position, address the ball using a baseball batter's stance, with the ball a few inches forward of your front foot. From here, stride into the ball as if you were swinging at a baseball, and hit the teed-up ball. Keep your stride relatively short—just long enough so the ball is straight across from your heel at impact. Notice how swinging in this manner enables you to lead with your hands and hold the angle.

Drill #21

Problem: Casting the club

If you're casting the club out away from you and making a sweeping motion through the impact zone, do this drill. Using an 8-iron, tee a ball up at least one inch high. Now swing at the ball, focusing on making a descending blow at the ball that catches the ball first, and then takes a divot after the tee. If you can take a divot after hitting the ball when it's teed up this high, you will have definitely held the angle properly and hit the ball with a descending blow.

Drill #22

Problem: Low swing plane

If you have an excessively low swing plane, hit some balls from a sidehill lie in which the ball is below your feet. To make crisp contact with the ball in this situation, you will have to make a more upright swing. Bear in mind that if you have short legs in relation to your upper body, you will naturally have a lower swing plane. In this situation, don't be overly concerned with trying to develop a more upright swing plane.

Drill #23

Problem: Low swing plane

Using an old club, take your address position with a wall two feet in back of you. Now take some practice swings, focusing on making sure the club never makes contact with the wall. Swing in a slower, more controlled manner at first until the more upright swing plane feels comfortable.

Drill #24

Problem: Excessively low follow-through

An excessively low follow-through often leads to a snap hook. To train yourself to make a higher follow-through, hit some shots where you let go of the club with your back hand at impact. This change will force you into a higher follow-through. Make sure you use a 10-finger grip when doing this drill to make it easier to let go of the club with your back hand. Also, make your first few swings nice and easy when doing this drill so your front shoulder can loosen up a little more.

Drill #25

Problem: Too upright of a swing plane

To remedy this problem, hit some shots from a sidehill lie in which the ball is above your feet. With the ball above your feet you will be forced to flatten out your swing plane to make clean contact with the ball.

Drill #26

Problem: Too upright of a swing plane

A quick drill you can do to help flatten out your swing plane is to take your normal address position over a ball, and then widen your stance by 12 inches. By widening your stance, you will need to flatten out your swing plane to make consistently solid contact with the ball. When you get to the point where you can make clean contact with the ball on every swing with this widened stance, narrow the stance by six inches, and hit some more balls.

4

Weight Shift

Drill #27

Problem: Excessive lower-body movement

If your legs are moving all over the place during your swing—a sure prescription for excessive shifting of your weight—do this drill. Take out your driver and tee up a ball. Now take your address position, only change it in one way. Instead of taking your normal lower-body set-up, bow your legs out as far as possible. Proceed to take a swing in which you keep your feet flat on the ground throughout your entire swing. The combination of bow-legged stance and flat-footed swing effectively take your lower body out of the equation, which should lead to more consistent shots.

Drill #28

Problem: Excessive lower-body movement

A simple way to quiet your lower body during your swing is to address a ball with your back foot raised up on tiptoe. This positioning should push about 90 percent of your weight to your front side. Now take a swing, making sure to keep your back foot raised up on its toes throughout the entire swing. Continue to hit balls in this manner until you develop a solid feel for what a quiet lower body feels like.

Drill #29

Problem: Excessive lower-body movement

A simple way to reduce the amount of movement in your lower body is to take some swings with your front foot turned in approximately 30 degrees. This stance will lock up your lower body and simplify your swing, which will add to your consistency.

Drill #30

Problem: Reverse weight shift

To help cure this problem, hold a club across the back of your shoulders and address a ball. Now swing back to the top of your backswing and stop. Your shoulders should have rotated 90 degrees, and the club should be behind the ball you have addressed. If it's not, check to see if your back leg has stiffened—the most common cause of a reverse weight shift.

Drill #31

Problem: Reverse weight shift

This drill offers a good way to get a visual idea of where your body and weight should be at the top of your backswing. Place a dowel rod or old club shaft in the ground so, at address, it is in line with your front shoulder and the ball. Now begin your swing, and stop at the top of your backswing. Check to make sure your front shoulder is behind the dowel rod at this point. If it's not, you've gotten into a reverse weight shift position.

Drill #32

Problem: Back leg stiffens, resulting in a reverse weight shift

A simple way to make sure you maintain some flex in your back leg is to hit some balls with your back foot turned in 30 to 45 degrees. With your foot in this position, any attempt to stiffen your back leg will result in you just about falling down, since a stiffening movement will send an excessive amount of weight to your front side.

Drill #33

Problem: Swaying

If your weight is moving out beyond the insides of your feet, hit some balls in which you stay flat-footed throughout the duration of the swing. This stance will force you to keep your weight centered, and help you to develop a better feel for where your weight should be when you're swinging.

Drill #34

Problem: Swaying

Without a club, take your address position about a foot from a wall. Next, rest your head against the wall (put a pillow or towel between your head and the wall to soften the contact). Now make a swing, making sure to keep your head against the pillow or towel throughout the entire swing. Doing this drill will keep your weight centered better, and help you develop a feel for not letting your weight sway.

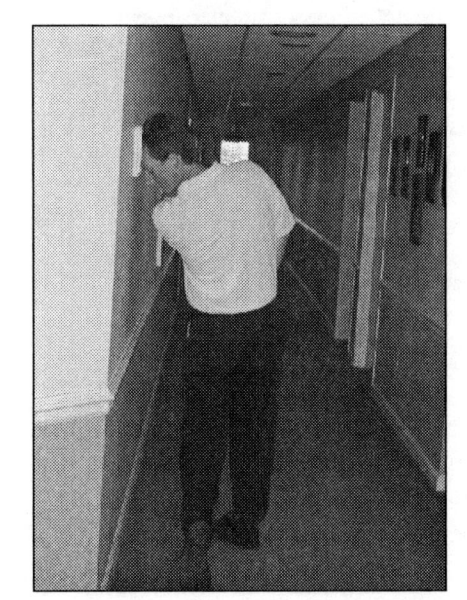

Drill #35

Problem: Swaying

Swaying occurs when you let your weight get to the outsides of your feet. To make sure you keep your weight on the insides of your feet, take some swings in which you turn both feet in at least 30 degrees. Swinging like this will lock up your lower body and keep your weight on the insides of your feet, and will also help you to develop a better feel for where your weight should be during your swing.

Drill #36

Problem: Swaying

Without a club, take your address position, and have a friend put his hand on your head. Your friend will hold your head in place while you make a swing. While making your swing, focus on producing a swing that rotates around your stabilized spine. When you swing around your spine, you are more apt to keep your weight inside your feet, which eliminates swaying.

Drill #37

Problem: Weight dives forward

When your weight dives forward during your swing, you will probably end up dragging the club behind your body, which costs you huge amounts of distance. To fix this swing flaw, take your address position, and then have a friend hold a club out so the grip is three inches forward of your head, just over your front shoulder. Now make a full swing, concentrating on making sure your head does not contact the club at any point.

Drill #38

Problem: Weight stays back after impact

Take your address position with your back heel raised off the ground. Next, make your normal swing, with one exception: try to have your back knee bump your front knee as the club passes through the impact zone. This movement will cause your weight to move forward as you pass through the impact zone, so your weight will be on your front side on the follow-through.

Drill #39

Problem: Weight stays back after impact

If your weight is staying back and your front hip is staying closed after impact, try this drill. Put a dowel rod or old club shaft in the ground eight feet down your target line. Now make your swing with one goal in mind: to have the ball pass to the left of the dowel rod after you hit it (if you're right-handed). To achieve this goal, you'll have to allow your front hip to open, and let your weight come forward in a better finished follow-through position.

Drill #40

Problem: Weight stays back after impact

Stare at a picture of a touring pro in his finished follow-through position until that image is etched in your mind. Now take a swing, and hold your pose in your finished follow-through position for three seconds, trying to emulate the pose of the picture you have in your head. If you can mimic that finished follow-through position, you will have moved your weight forward onto your front side.

Drill #41

Problem: Weight stays back after impact

When golfers fail to get their weight forward after impact, it's often because they casted the club away from their body during the downswing and made a sweeping motion with the club through the impact zone. This movement costs the golfer a tremendous amount of distance. To correct that problem, place a clubhead cover on the ground one foot behind the ball you are about to hit. Now swing, focusing on making contact with the ball without touching the clubhead cover. To do this, you will have to properly transfer your weight forward, and hold the angle better.

Drill #42

Problem: Poor balance throughout swing

To force yourself to maintain good balance while you swing, take some practice swings while standing on top of two turned-over range buckets. Any excessive weight shifts or swaying will quickly cause you to lose your balance. Maintain your balance properly, however, and you will stay comfortably on top of the buckets.

Drill #43

Problem: Poor balance throughout swing

Golfers often overswing—and therefore get out of balance—because they don't understand exactly what the body is supposed to do during the swing. They are under the impression that the body has a lot of work to do in the swing, so they add excess movements into their swing. To get a feel for how little the body needs to do during the swing, fold your arms across your chest and make some swings. Take notice of how little your body does when swinging in this manner. This kind of quiet, balanced body is exactly what you need when making your normal swing with a club.

5

Impact Position

Drill #44

Problem: Right elbow flies out away from body at impact

Letting your right elbow fly out away from your body at impact can lead to some pretty ugly pushes and slices. To train your right elbow to stay close to your body at impact (if you're right-handed), take some swings with only your right arm, swinging the clubhead through at knee level. This drill will force your elbow to stay in close to your body, and it will also help you to get a better feel for a proper release.

Drill #45

Problem: Raising up at impact

When you raise your body up at impact, you hit a lot of thin shots. To help train yourself not to come up, address a ball in your normal manner. Place another ball two inches outside the ball you are addressing. Now make your swing, but instead of hitting the ball you addressed, hit the ball that is two inches to the outside of the addressed ball. You must stay down to make contact with that ball.

Drill #46

Problem: Diving down at ball at impact

To keep yourself from diving down at the ball and hitting a lot of fat shots, put a golf ball under the toes of each foot as you address a ball. Now make your swing. The balls under your toes will keep your weight more on your heels, and hinder your efforts to dive down.

Drill #47

Problem: Diving down at ball at impact

Take your normal address position over a ball with another ball placed two inches to the inside of the ball you are addressing. Now make a swing, but instead of hitting the ball you addressed, hit the ball that is two inches inside of it. To make solid contact with that ball, you will have to make sure you maintain your spine angle. If you try to dive down into the inside ball, you will probably hit a few inches behind it.

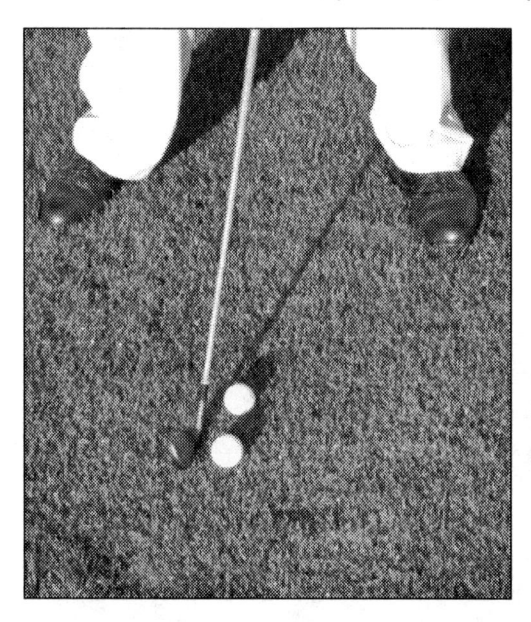

Drill #48

Problem: Diving forward at impact

Using an old club, take your address position six inches away from a wall that is just beyond your front foot. Take a smooth easy swing into the wall, making sure your hands and shoulder do not make contact with the wall. If they do make contact with the wall, you're still diving forward. If you don't have an old club to use with this drill, use some tape or a rubber band to attach a piece of cloth to your clubhead to keep your club from getting scratched.

Drill #49

Problem: Taking huge divots

Taking huge divots is usually the result of approaching the ball from too steep of a swing angle. This simple drill will help you develop a better feel for making more of a sweeping swing through the impact zone. Start by placing your clubhead on the ground just behind your back foot. The clubhead should be just to the inside of your target line, and the clubface should be slightly open. From this position, drag the clubhead along the ground through the impact zone, making sure to close the clubface as you do so. After the clubhead passes your front foot, complete your release and follow through in your normal manner.

Drill #50

Problem: Flipping wrists at the ball at impact

Flipping your wrists at the ball costs you distance, accuracy, and consistency. To develop a better feel for not flipping your wrists, hit some bump-and-run shots using the following method: Using a 5-iron, take your address position with your feet a few inches closer together than normal, and your front foot opened up slightly. The ball should be positioned just behind the center of your stance. When you make your swing, make a steeper swing, focusing on keeping your hands in front of the ball at impact. Finally, you want to make a shorter, more abbreviated follow-through, trying to keep your hands ahead of the clubhead for as long as possible after impact.

A properly struck bump-and-run shot will produce a shot with a lower trajectory, which is what you're aiming for. If that's what you get, you're definitely not flipping your wrists at the ball.

6

Release

Drill #51

Problem: Not releasing fully

To get the proper feel of what a full release feels like, take some swings with your back arm only, swinging the club through at knee level. Make five to ten swings in a row without stopping to help you get used to making a full, rhythmic release.

Drill #52

Problem: Not releasing fully

Without a club, assume your normal address position, making sure your thumbs are pointing straight to the ground. Now swing back to waist-high in your backswing and stop. Your thumbs should be pointing straight up. Now swing through to waist-high in your follow-through. If you've fully released your hands and forearms, your thumbs should again be pointing straight up.

Drill #53

Problem: Not releasing fully

To really force yourself to make a full and proper release, get an old club and make a swing where you let go of the club just after impact in an attempt to throw the club straight down your target line. If you can throw the club straight down your target line, you can make a perfect release. To further enhance the benefits of this drill, get someone to videotape you throwing the club. The camera will reveal an absolutely perfect release, and prove to you that you can release fully.

Drill #54

Problem: Poor release

A simple way to make sure you complete your release is to take your address position with your right index finger (if you're right-handed) pointing straight down the shaft of your club. Now make some easy practice swings, stopping at waist-high on your follow-through. If you have released the club properly, your index finger will be pointing straight down your target line.

Drill #55

Problem: Poor release

An easy way to check to see if you are releasing the club properly is to stick a tee in the end of your grip and make some half swings. Swing to waist-high in your follow-through. If you've released properly, the tee will be pointing to the ground again.

Drill #56

Problem: Poor release

One of the simplest ways to improve your release is to take some swings with a broom. The extra weight and resistance of the broom will force you to fully release your hands and forearms as you swing the broom through the impact zone and make your follow-through.

Drill #57

Problem: Poor extension after impact

Stick a tee in the ground four inches in front of a ball you are addressing. The tee should stick one inch out of the ground. Using a long-iron, swing at the ball, with your goal being to get good extension and knock the tee out of the ground.

Drill #58

Problem: Poor extension after impact

To force yourself to extend your arms just after passing through the impact zone, get your driver out and address a teed-up ball. After you get set and ready to swing, move six inches to your right (if you're right-handed) so the ball is out beyond your left foot. Now make your swing. To make solid contact with the ball, you will have to get full extension on your swing.

Drill #59

Problem: Excessive release leading to snap hooks

If you release too much and too quickly, try this drill to get a feel for a proper release. Take your grip on the club with your right hand on top of your left hand (if you're right-handed). This kind of grip will quiet down your right hand and get your hands to work together better. Take plenty of practice swings this way to develop the feel for a proper release.

Drill #60

Problem: Not releasing fully

To help get yourself to release the club more fully as you pass through the impact zone, make some swings, with your only swing thought being that you are going to throw the clubhead at the ball with your right hand (if you're right-handed). This aggressive swing thought—used by many baseball players to make sure they explode into the ball—should aid you in getting a full release.

Drill #61

Problem: Not releasing fully

A simple swing key you can use to get yourself to release better is to tell yourself before each swing that you are going to have the toe of the clubhead pass through the impact zone before the heel of the club does. By focusing on trying to get the toe to pass the heel, you will be much more likely to attain a proper release.

7

General

Drill #62

Problem: Poor rhythm

When golfers have poor rhythm, it's often because they become so focused on the ball that they forget about their swing. To help you make smooth, rhythmic swings in which the ball simply gets in the way of your swing, tee up a ball and address it with your pitching wedge. Just before you begin your backswing, close your eyes, then make your swing. By closing your eyes, all of your focus will be directed towards simply making a good swing, and your rhythm should improve.

Drill #63

Problem: Poor rhythm

This tough but fun drill will help you get your entire body working together as one unit. Using your driver, take a full swing at a ball, but try to hit the ball only 100 yards. Make sure you don't shorten your backswing or follow-through, simply slow down your tempo. To hit the ball only 100 yards, your body will have to work as a single, smooth unit.

After you get to where you can consistently hit your driver just 100 yards, try to hit some 150 yards. Again, focus on a smooth, rhythmic swing. When you can consistently hit your driver 150 yards, go back to trying to hit the ball just 100 yards again. If you can do that, you will have gone a long way towards developing excellent rhythm.

Drill #64

Problem: Poor rhythm

If you tend to tense up when you make your swing, try this drill to help you gain a feel for making a fluid swing. Hit some balls in your normal manner, taking the time to notice how the swing feels. After half a dozen normal swings, put your club aside and take your address position with your arms hanging loosely down and your fingers relaxed and extended. From this position, make some practice swings, focusing on how easy and fluid this swing feels. Once this relaxed swing feels normal and comfortable, hit some balls, with your sole goal being to copy this fluid swing.

Drill #65

Problem: Poor rhythm

To help develop a swing that has more rhythm and gets your entire body working together, do this drill. Hold your 4-iron in one hand and your 5-iron in the other, and make some swings, focusing on making sure the clubs never bump into each other. If you can make full swings like this without the clubs touching, your body will be working as a single unit.

Drill #66

Problem: Poor rhythm

To get yourself in the right frame of mind for making a more rhythmic swing, view your golf swing as a dance step. An easy way to do that is to silently call out your steps as you make your swing. Keep it a simple "one…and…two." Say "one" as you begin your take-away, "and" as you reach the top of your backswing, and "two" as you reach the impact zone. Say the words rhythmically, and your swing should follow.

Drill #67

Problem: Poor rhythm

A simple swing thought you can use to improve your swing rhythm is to say "smooooth" to yourself just as you begin your swing. Stretch the word out to really stress to your mind and body the importance of making a relaxed, rhythmic swing.

Drill #68

Problem: Swinging too hard

To slow down your swing and help you stay within yourself, hit some balls out of a fairway bunker without digging your feet into the sand. Trying to swing hard from this position will quickly get you out of balance, leaving you with no chance of making clean contact with the ball.

Drill #69

Problem: Swinging too hard

Using your driver, hit ten balls 75 yards. To do this, you will want to take swings that are shorter and easier than normal. You will probably be surprised at how easy of a swing you will have to take to make sure the ball only travels 75 yards. After hitting that group of ten shots, hit ten balls 100 yards. Follow that up with ten shots hit 125 yards, ten hit 150 yards, and ten hit 175 yards.

By the time you get to the last set of ten, you should have noticed that an easy and compact swing is all that is needed to hit the ball a fairly long distance. With this newfound knowledge, you will feel more comfortable in taking easier swings at the ball.

Drill #70

Problem: Swinging too hard

Using a mid-iron, address a ball, then move two feet back from the ball and take a smooth, relaxed practice swing. Then move six inches closer to your ball and take another smooth practice swing. Move another six inches closer and take another relaxed swing, then move six inches closer still and take a fourth easy, fluid practice swing. Finally, move back to the ball you initially addressed and take another smooth swing, focusing on repeating the same swing you've just taken four times, this time allowing the ball to get in the way of your swing. You will be surprised at how far an easy swing will hit the ball.

Drill #71

Problem: Swinging too hard

Take some practice swings where you swing at only 90 percent of your normal speed. Once that feels comfortable, take some swings where you swing at only 75 percent of your normal speed. After that 75-percent swing feels comfortable, hit some shots where you try to mimic that 75-percent swing speed. You will not only notice that the ball is flying just about as far as it normally does, but that you are much more accurate with this 75-percent swing speed.

Drill #72

Problem: Lack of swing speed

To increase your swing speed and build up forearm, wrist, and hand strength, take plenty of one-handed swings with both hands. Focus on trying to get the club to make a whoosh sound as it passes through the impact zone. As your strength and swing speed increase, try to get louder and louder whoosh sounds.

Drill #73

Problem: Lack of swing speed

Start from the top of your backswing, except have the club resting across your shoulders instead of up and away from your body. From this starting point, make your swing. By starting your swing with the club across your shoulders in a stagnant position, you won't be able to use the momentum of your backswing to carry you through the impact zone. This drill will teach you to explode into the ball and will help you build up the muscles needed to do that.

Drill #74

Problem: Poor long-iron play

The most common problem golfers face when hitting long-iron shots is that they swing too hard in an effort to maximize distance and to help get the ball in the air. To get a better feel for the kind of swing you should make with your long-irons, take out your 3-iron and make some practice swings with your goal being to simply clip the top of the grass as you pass through the impact zone. Notice how it is easier to clip the top of the grass when you make a slower, more rhythmic swing. This kind of swing is what you want to take when actually hitting a ball with your long-irons.

Drill #75

Problem: Topping the ball

Using a mid-iron, tee a ball up one to one-and-a-half inches. Swing with the sole goal of breaking the tee in half—don't worry at all about where the ball goes. When you get to where you can consistently hit the tee, lower the ball so it's only teed up about half an inch, and again focus only on trying to break the tee in half.

After you can routinely hit the tee with the ball teed up only half an inch, put the ball on the ground. Begin to hit balls off the ground, viewing the ball as merely another tee that you are going to try to break in half.

Drill #76

Problem: Shanking

Place a tee one to one-and-a-half inches outside of a ball you have addressed, and hit the ball without making any contact with the tee. To hit the ball without hitting the tee, you will have to refrain from reaching out at the ball and hitting the ball off the hosel.

Drill #77

Problem: Good swing with poor accuracy

To help you zero in on your target, narrow your focus. Instead of focusing on the green as you prepare to hit an approach shot, focus on a small branch of a tree just behind the green that you will aim at. Or better yet, pick out a leaf on that branch as your target. You can refine this focusing ability by picking out a different target on each shot you make on the driving range. Aim for a flagstick on one shot, the extreme edge of a bunker on another, and the television antenna on a house that's beyond the practice range with the following shot. By narrowing your focus, you will improve your accuracy.

PART II

Short-Game Drills

8

Around the Green

Drill #78

Problem: Poor touch on chip shots

To help improve your touch on chip shots, take a bag of balls to a spot five or ten feet off a green and select a hole that you will chip to. Now place three paper plates on the green. The first one should be right at the edge of the green, along the path you want your shot to travel, with the second plate five feet beyond the first plate, and the third plate five feet beyond the second plate. Begin to hit chip shots in which you alternate the plate you are trying to hit with each swing. Use the same club for each shot, and attempt to hit the plates on the fly. By changing the distance goal of each shot, while still trying to get the ball close to the hole, you will begin to develop better touch.

Drill #79

Problem: Poor touch on chip shots

Using tees, make an eight-foot diameter circle on a chipping green. You don't need to have a hole in the middle of the circle. Proceed to hit chip shots, with your goal being to get the ball to stop somewhere within the circle. Being able to consistently get a ball to stop within a circle of this size means you will often have no more than a three- or four-foot putt to save par.

Drill #80

Problem: Too much weight shift on chip shots

To be consistent on chip shots, you need to have a simple swing, which means keeping the majority of your weight on your front foot throughout your entire swing. To make sure you keep your weight on your front foot, make some chips with your back foot raised up on tiptoe. This stance will force you to keep the majority of your weight on your front foot, which will simplify your swing and improve your chipping skills.

Drill #81

Problem: Poor swing path on chip shots

Your swing on chip shots should be as simple as possible. Part of keeping the swing simple is to take the club straight back and through as you hit the ball. To make sure you do this, place two clubs on the ground parallel to your target line. Put a club on either side of your ball, with each club about two inches from your ball. Proceed to make some swings, focusing on making solid contact with the ball while avoiding making any contact with the clubs.

Drill #82

Problem: Flipping wrists on chip shots

To make sure your wrists stay cocked as you pass through the impact zone on your chip shots, try this drill. Set up to hit a very short chip shot (10 to 15 feet is long enough). While you take your address position, have a friend gently press the grip of one of his clubs into the ground about three inches in front of the ball you are about to hit. Proceed to hit your chip shot, allowing your friend's club to stop your swing. If you are making a good swing and not flipping your wrists at the ball, your hands will be ahead of the clubhead at this stopping point.

Drill #83

Problem: Poor touch on chip and pitch shots

Toss 10 balls around a green so they are various distances away from the green and your intended target hole. Using just one club, proceed to hit all 10 balls to your target hole. By using the same club for each shot regardless of distance, lie, and the amount of green you have to work with, you will be forced to develop better touch to get your shots close to the hole.

Drill #84

Problem: Inconsistency getting up and down from around the green

Play 18 holes of chip/pitch-and-putt from around a chipping green. Start your holes from six inches to 60 feet off the green, and use as many clubs as you want to get the ball in the hole. Play each hole as a par three. To help keep you focused, set a target score before you begin. Once you attain your target score, lower it for the next time you do the drill.

Drill #85

Problem: Taking club back inside on pitch shots

To help train yourself to take the club back on an outside-to-inside swing path on your pitch shots, place a dowel rod or old club shaft two feet out from your back foot at address. Now take your swing. If you try to take your club back inside the target line, your club will contact the dowel rod/club shaft.

Drill #86

Problem: Excessive release on follow-through on pitch shots

You don't need to make a full release on pitch shots and this drill will make sure you don't. Place a dowel rod or old club shaft two feet out from your front foot as you take your address over a ball. Proceed to hit your pitch shot, focusing on making sure your club doesn't make contact with the dowel rod/club shaft as you make your follow-through.

Drill #87

Problem: Poor concept of how to hit greenside bunker shots

To get a better idea of the path your clubhead should take through the sand when hitting out of a greenside bunker, draw two parallel lines six inches apart in the sand. Address the lines so they are centered around your front heel. Proceed to make a swing where your club enters the sand just inside the back line and exits the sand just inside the front line—the approximate distance your club should take through the sand. After making your swing, move up the line a foot or two, and make another swing, again trying to enter the sand just inside the back line and exit just inside the front line. Continue along the entire length of the line, repeating the process.

Drill #88

Problem: Fear of letting the clubhead enter the sand when in greenside bunkers

Many golfers have a phobia about letting their clubhead enter the sand when blasting out of a greenside bunker, so they try to pick the ball out of the bunker, which is a tricky and inconsistent way to go about your sand play. To get over this phobia, tee up a ball in a bunker so the head of the tee sticks out of the sand about half an inch. Now take your swing, with your sole goal being to try to break the tee in half. Don't worry about where the ball goes while you develop the ability to break the tee on a consistent basis. As you will soon find out, when you do break the tee, you will usually hit a good shot.

When you get to where you can break the tee on a regular basis, remove the tee and hit some regular bunker shots. If it helps, pretend that you are still trying to break a tee that is just under the ball.

Drill #89

Problem: Poor bunker play

A simple way to improve your bunker play is to make a footprint in the sand, place a ball in the middle of the footprint, and simply try to erase the footprint with your swing. Don't worry at all about the ball—your sole focus is trying to remove the footprint from the sand. If you can erase it nicely, you will hit a good shot.

9

Putting

Drill #90

Problem: Poor touch

To improve your touch on the green, take five to ten balls out to the putting green, and putt the first anywhere from eight to sixty feet. Proceed to hit the rest of the balls to the first one you putted, striving to get the balls to stop as close as possible to the first ball. After you've hit all the balls, repeat the process, being sure to vary the distance with each group of balls you putt.

Drill #91

Problem: Poor touch on long putts

Using some tees, make a five-foot diameter circle on the practice green. Now make some long putts towards the circle, attempting to have each putt stop within the circle. The length of the putts should vary from 20 to 80 feet.

Drill #92

Problem: Poor swing path

To help develop a proper swing path on your putts, lay two clubs on the ground, one of them half an inch outside the toe of your putterhead, and the other half an inch from the heel of your putterhead. The clubs should be parallel to your target line. Stroke some putts, focusing on not making any contact with either of the clubs.

Drill #93

Problem: Not keeping putterhead squared at impact

Find a place on a green where you can attempt four-foot putts without any break, and without putting uphill or downhill. From this position, address a four-foot putt, but instead of stroking it in the hole with your normal swing, sweep the ball into the hole without taking a backswing. If you have your putterhead squared up properly to the hole, the ball will go in.

Drill #94

Problem: Trouble reading sidehill putts

To learn how to read sidehill putts better, take five balls out to a putting green, and leave your putter in the bag. Find a spot where you can have a breaking putt of five to sixty feet, and roll each of the five balls to the hole, taking time to notice how much the putts break. After rolling the five balls to the hole, find another breaking putt on the green and repeat the process. By rolling the balls instead of putting them, you remove any anxiety you might have over trying to hole the putt. You can simply focus on reading the putt, and you get a chance to watch the putt from directly behind the ball, rather than over the top of it. This vantage point should aid you in reading the sidehill putts better.

Drill #95

Problem: Poor concentration when putting

To improve your focus on the green, take some time to putt towards a tee. By putting to such a small target, you will be forced to focus more on the target, which will quickly improve your concentration.

Drill #96

Problem: Poor direction on putts

To develop better and more consistent direction with your putts, putt three putts in a row from two to three feet away from a hole. With the first putt, attempt to curl it in on the left side of the hole. With the second putt, knock it in the middle of the cup. With the last putt, curl it in on the right side of the hole. Being able to successfully complete this drill on a consistent basis will help your putting direction immensely.

Drill #97

Problem: Jabbing at short putts

Typically, a golfer will jab at a short, normally easy putt because he is nervous and tense about the possibility of missing the putt. To help conquer this nervousness, do the following drill. After you have completed your normal putting practice, begin to putt two-footers. As soon as you make 25 consecutive two-footers, you can leave the putting green. While this task may seem simple, you will notice that when you get to the point where you have made 20 to 22 straight putts, you will begin to get nervous—you don't want your last few minutes of work to have gone to waste. And you don't want to be stuck on the putting green all day. At this point, you will have to overcome your nerves to make a smooth putting stroke that will get the ball in the bottom of the cup.

Drill #98

Problem: Decelerating on putts

To make sure you properly accelerate through the ball on your putts, address some putts in the four- to eight-foot range and place a tee in the ground four inches behind the ball you are about to hit. Now stroke the putt, making sure you don't make any contact with the tee. By taking an abbreviated backswing, you will be forced to accelerate the putterhead through the ball as you move it through the impact zone.

Drill #99

Problem: Looking up on putts

To force yourself to focus on the back edge of the ball until after you have made contact, putt some four- to six-foot putts with your sand wedge. Since the front edge of the sand wedge will need to touch the center of the ball to attain solid contact, you will be forced to keep your head down. Once this stroke feels comfortable, go back to your putter and repeat this head-down stroke.

Drill #100

Problem: Wrists break down on putting stroke

To get a feel for keeping your wrists firm throughout your putting stroke, do this simple drill. Without your putter, let your arms hang straight down, and then bring your palms together to form a triangle between your arms and shoulders. Using your shoulders, swing your arms back and forth to simulate a solid, one-piece putting stroke.

Drill #101

Problem: Tense putting stroke

To help develop a feel for a more relaxed putting stroke, putt to another ball rather than to a hole. Putting to a ball should help relieve the tension of trying to hole out the putt, allowing you to make a more fluid stroke.

About the Authors

Glenn Berggoetz is the teaching professional at Custom Golf of New Haven in New Haven, Indiana.

PGA professional **Alan Moyer** is the head golf professional at Willow Bend Country Club in Van Wert, Ohio.